# The Tet Offensive

### by Mary Englar

Content Adviser: John Guilmartin Jr., Ph.D.,
Department of History,
Ohio State University

Reading Adviser: Alexa L. Sandmann, Ed.D.,
Professor of Literacy, College and Graduate School of Education,
Kent State University

Compass Point Books ✦ Minneapolis, Minnesota

Compass Point Books
151 Good Counsel Drive
P.O. Box 669
Mankato, MN 56002-0669

 This book was manufactured with paper containing at least 10 percent post-consumer waste.

On the cover: U.S. armored vehicles rolled through Saigon during the Tet Offensive.

Photographs ©: Bettmann/Corbis, cover, 4, 9, 20, 29, 34; Prints Old & Rare, back cover (far left); Library of Congress, back cover; AP Images, 6, 12, 17, 30, 35; Time & Life Pictures/Getty Images, 11, 28, 37; National Archives and Records Administration, 14; Bill Ingraham/AP Images, 15; Pictorial Parade/Getty Images, 18; Getty Images, 21, 39; AFP/Getty Images, 23; Tim Page/Corbis, 24; DVIC/NARA, 32; LBJ Library photo by Yoichi R. Okamoto, 40.

Editor: Julie Gassman
Page Production: Bobbie Nuytten
Photo Researcher: Robert McConnell
Cartographer: XNR Productions, Inc.
Library Consultant: Kathleen Baxter

Art Director: LuAnn Ascheman-Adams
Creative Director: Keith Griffin
Editorial Director: Nick Healy
Managing Editor: Catherine Neitge

**Library of Congress Cataloging-in-Publication Data**
Englar, Mary.
  The Tet Offensive / by Mary Englar.
     p. cm. — (We the people)
  Includes index.
  ISBN 978-0-7565-3844-6 (library binding)
1. Tet Offensive, 1968—Juvenile literature.
  I. Title. II. Series.
  DS557.8.T4E54 2007
  959.704'342—dc22                    2008005734

Visit Compass Point Books on the Internet at *www.compasspointbooks.com*
or e-mail your request to *custserv@compasspointbooks.com*

# TABLE OF CONTENTS

# SAIGON ATTACKED!

Early on the morning of January 31, 1968, a team of guerrillas met secretly in Saigon, the capital of South Vietnam. After months of planning, their leader finally revealed their mission. The rebels were ordered to attack the U.S. Embassy in the city.

The 19 guerrillas belonged to the Viet Cong, a

*The U.S. Embassy in Saigon, with its rooftop helicopter landing port, opened just a few months before the Tet Offensive.*

communist group that opposed the South Vietnamese government. The Viet Cong wanted the U.S. armed forces, who supported the South Vietnamese, to leave the country. Preparing for their mission, the rebels gathered their weapons and climbed into a taxi and a truck.

An 8-foot (2.4-meter) wall surrounded the embassy grounds. That morning, two military police (MPs) guarded the night gate. When the Viet Cong arrived, they fired their guns at the MPs. The MPs fired back and locked the steel gate. Using their radios, they reported the attack.

Moments later, an explosion knocked a 3-foot (1-m) hole in the outer wall. One of the MPs called headquarters. "They're coming in! Help me!" he shouted into the radio. The Viet Cong killed both MPs. They ran toward the main embassy building in the center of the grounds. Only three Marines guarded the building. Six American employees worked upstairs.

The Marines in the lobby heard the explosion and ran to lock the front door. The Viet Cong launched three

*Two MPs were killed within minutes of the first attack.*

rockets at the embassy door. Two smashed through the wall
and exploded in the lobby. One Marine was knocked down,
and the other was badly wounded. On the roof, the third
Marine fired at the Viet Cong as they came through the
outer wall. When his shotgun jammed, he emptied his
pistol at them.

6

## ABOUT THE WAR

The Vietnam War was fought from 1959 to 1975. South Vietnam battled the communist Viet Cong of the South and the communists of North Vietnam. (Communists believe in an economic system in which goods and property are owned by the government and shared in common. Communist rulers limit personal freedoms to achieve their goals.)

The Viet Cong and the North Vietnamese wanted to unite the two countries into one communist nation. They were backed by the Soviet Union and China. The United States supported the South Vietnamese with money and troops. The first American combat troops arrived in 1965. By 1967, there were more than 500,000 U.S. troops fighting in Vietnam.

The fighting grew costly in lives and money. Protests against the war increased. In 1973, a cease-fire agreement was reached, and U.S. troops were withdrawn. Fighting continued, however, until 1975, when the North took control of a united Vietnam.

The war killed more than 58,000 Americans and between 2 million and 4 million Vietnamese. More than 300,000 Americans were wounded during the war, the longest in U.S. history. The effects of the long, bloody war are still felt today.

In the lobby, a Marine checked on his wounded friend. Both of their radios had been destroyed. The Marine on the roof tried to reach the lobby guards on his radio. When there was no answer, he feared the Viet Cong were inside the embassy building. He used his radio to report that the guerrillas were inside.

The Viet Cong did not know how many guards were inside. The guerrilla leaders had been killed coming through the wall, so the others did not have complete orders. They decided to defend their position on the grounds, and they never broke into the embassy building.

Reports of the attack sped around Saigon: The U.S. Embassy was under siege. Only 15 minutes after the first attack, an American news reporter sent the first story to New York City. No one knew the exact details. The evening news programs in the United States inaccurately reported that Viet Cong guerrillas had taken over the embassy building.

Military police responded to the call for help. They found the night gate locked. When they tried to look inside,

8

*Once inside the gate, the MPs and other soldiers surrounded the building and searched for the Viet Cong.*

the Viet Cong fired at them. The MPs retreated. Some climbed to the roofs of nearby buildings and fired into the grounds. A rescue helicopter tried to land on the roof at 5 A.M. Heavy gunfire from the Viet Cong forced the pilot to turn back.

At dawn, the MPs shot off the lock on the front gate and stormed into the grounds. They tracked down the guerrillas and killed or wounded all of them. More U.S. soldiers landed on the roof and searched the embassy building floor by floor.

Dozens of journalists entered the embassy grounds while the MPs searched for the guerrillas. Dead and wounded Viet Cong lay near the embassy building. The MP guards lay dead at the side gate. The reporters sent film and photographs of the scene back to the United States.

At 9:15 A.M., six hours after the first call for help, the embassy building and grounds were declared secure. A few minutes later, General William C. Westmoreland, commander of U.S. armed forces in South Vietnam, arrived. After a tour of the grounds, he stopped to talk to reporters. Westmoreland did not appear worried. "The enemy's well-laid plans went afoul," he declared. All the enemy guerrillas had been killed or captured.

The following day, American television and newspapers reported on the attack in further detail. Before this battle, most Americans had believed Westmoreland and

*Journalists, accompanied by MPs and embassy staff, photographed the dead Viet Cong fighters.*

President Lyndon Johnson when they had said the Vietnam War was going well. If the war was going well, though, how had the enemy entered the U.S. Embassy so easily? Some Americans began to question their leaders.

As the news reports came in, Americans learned that

**11**

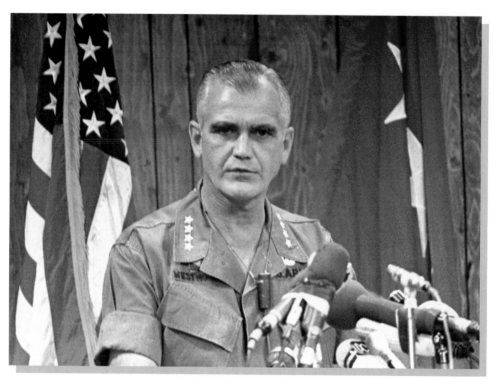

*Following the attack on the embassy, General Westmoreland told reporters about the other attacks that had taken place throughout Vietnam.*

the communists had also attacked more than 100 South Vietnamese cities. These daring attacks, launched during the Vietnamese New Year holiday of Tet, killed many civilians and soldiers. Over the next few months, the attacks became known as the Tet Offensive.

# A DANGEROUS ENEMY

When the Tet Offensive started, the United States had been fighting in South Vietnam for almost three years. American soldiers were trained to meet their enemies on an open battlefield. They fought with tanks, artillery, and warplanes. Then they moved on to the next battle. Together with the Army of the Republic of [South] Vietnam (ARVN), they won most battles on open ground.

The North Vietnam Army (NVA) and Viet Cong had nearly as many soldiers as the United States and South Vietnam. However, the Viet Cong lacked tanks, artillery, and planes. In face-to-face battles, the Viet Cong lost many soldiers. They preferred surprise guerrilla attacks. They attacked with mortars and guns, and then melted back into the jungle.

The guerrillas planted mines and traps along the jungle trails. When the Americans searched the jungles, many were killed by mines. Guerrilla war forced the Americans to fight

13

*The Viet Cong dug holes and filled them with punji-stakes—sharpened bamboo spikes. The holes were often concealed so the victims would unknowingly step into them.*

small battles in many places, resulting in higher casualties.

In the United States, the number of dead and wounded was reported on the evening news almost every night. Americans watched film of the battles in the jungles and fields of Vietnam. Though the Viet Cong lost more soldiers, the U.S. troops never seemed to win. In addition, from 1965 onward, the Viet Cong were joined by increasing numbers of NVA soldiers. By the summer of 1967, roughly half of the Americans in a poll said they were not sure they understood the war. Many said they wondered whether the war could be won.

*As the war went on, more and more Americans opposed it.*

North Vietnam's leaders also wondered whether there was a way to win the war. In the summer of 1967, they believed that the war was a stalemate. As long as the American troops defended South Vietnam, they thought, North Vietnam could not win.

The Viet Cong and North Vietnamese leaders agreed on a risky plan. They would attack South Vietnam during the Vietnamese national holiday of Tet in 1968. Tet, which is the most important holiday in Vietnam, celebrates the lunar New Year. Most Vietnamese people spend the holiday visiting relatives and honoring their ancestors.

For the first three years of the war, both sides had agreed to cease-fires during the holidays of Christmas, New Year's, and Tet. If the communists attacked during the cease-fire, their leaders thought, many ARVN soldiers would be away from their bases. Plus, they hoped to catch the Americans by surprise.

# A Secret Communist Plan

North Vietnam's General Vo Nguyen Giap planned the Tet attacks. He began to send weapons and NVA troops to help the Viet Cong. The soldiers carried guns, artillery shells, and ammunition south on the Ho Chi Minh Trail.

The trail was a series of paths along Vietnam's borders with Laos and Cambodia. It was a dangerous route for the North Vietnamese. American planes often bombed the trail. Despite the dangers, the U.S. military estimated that 20,000 NVA soldiers a month entered South Vietnam in 1967.

General Giap needed high numbers of NVA soldiers in South Vietnam to carry out his plan. More

*The Ho Chi Minh Trail wound through jungles and mountains.*

17

than 100 of South Vietnam's cities would be attacked. He told his officers to prepare for a great battle to defeat the Americans. He said their victory would bring freedom and independence to all of Vietnam.

*General Vo Nguyen Giap*

In the fall of 1967, General Westmoreland received reports of unusual communist military activity. The reports warned of a big battle, but they did not give a date. Some reports warned of Viet Cong attacks on South Vietnam's cities. The Viet Cong had never attacked large cities before, so few American military or

18

embassy officials believed the warnings. Even if the reports were true, they thought, the communist forces would be spread thin. And they thought that when the Americans struck back, they would destroy the NVA and Viet Cong.

General Westmoreland believed that the NVA planned to invade the northern provinces of South Vietnam. In 1967, more than half of U.S. troops were stationed in the north. Reports of large NVA troop movements near the northern border convinced Westmoreland he was right.

On the morning of January 21, 1968, the first NVA strike came. The Khe Sanh U.S. military base in the northern mountains came under heavy artillery attack. About 6,000 American and ARVN troops defended the base. Westmoreland estimated that 20,000 to 40,000 NVA troops had surrounded Khe Sanh, blocking the only road.

The first attack destroyed most of the base's ammunition. An enemy shell struck stored ammunition. When it exploded, the blast damaged helicopters and the runway. With the road blocked, the troops at Khe Sanh

*Bunkers reinforced with sandbags helped protect the Marines at Khe Sanh.*

could get supplies only by air. They dug in to wait for a ground attack.

Westmoreland believed that the NVA troops planned for a long battle in the northern provinces of South Vietnam. Historians are not sure why they attacked Khe Sanh first. After the war, General Giap said he had hoped the Americans would send more troops to the north. That way fewer American soldiers would have been left to protect the cities in the south when his communist troops attacked during Tet.

# ATTACKS THROUGHOUT SOUTH VIETNAM

While Khe Sanh was under fire, the Viet Cong and NVA continued planning the Tet Offensive. The Viet Cong led the first attacks just after midnight on January 30, 1968. Their leaders believed that NVA troops would arrive to

*In many places, the initial attacks were mounted by the Viet Cong without NVA support.*

help them once they took the cities. NVA officers told them to expect sympathetic South Vietnamese civilians and soldiers to rise up and join them.

The Viet Cong attacked eight cities that night. More than 2,000 Viet Cong attacked Ban Me Thuot, a city in the Central Highlands. The city was destroyed, and civilians fled to churches to hide from the fighting.

Early the next morning, reports of the attacks reached Westmoreland at his headquarters in Saigon. After talking to his officers, Westmoreland ordered an end to the Tet cease-fire. His officers agreed that more attacks were likely. The American and ARVN troops were ordered to be on maximum alert.

Around 3 A.M. on January 31, the communist forces hit more than 100 cities and villages in South Vietnam. The attacks targeted ARVN headquarters, radio stations, and police stations. The Viet Cong took over some radio stations but were unable to broadcast their liberation message. The ARVN had disabled the stations before they left.

*A female Viet Cong soldier wields a rocket-propelled grenade in an attack in the far south.*

In some cities, the communist forces were pushed back quickly. They lost thousands of soldiers, and they did not hold the cities. Still, the surprise attacks shocked the Americans and the South Vietnamese. Before the Tet Offensive, many South Vietnamese civilians had fled the countryside to escape the fighting. Most southerners had felt safer in cities. After the attacks, the South Vietnamese did not feel safe anywhere.

*Many Saigon residents fled the city to escape the violence.*

No people were more surprised than those in Saigon. More than 4,000 Viet Cong had entered Saigon just before Tet. They had smuggled in weapons in vegetable carts, baskets of rice, and loads of firewood. Then they had hidden the weapons in houses near the attack targets.

During the evening of January 30, teams of 10 to 15 Viet Cong met in many parts of the capital. Their targets would be the Presidential Palace, the U.S. Embassy, a radio station, and the police stations. The teams prepared their weapons and waited until the middle of the night.

At 3 A.M., as in other cities, the Viet Cong attacked throughout Saigon. Some teams were able to capture their targets. The U.S. Embassy and the radio station were two of the successes. In contrast, the attack on the Presidential Palace was quickly shut down, and the Viet Cong were forced to take cover in an apartment building nearby.

At the same time, the U.S. military bases near Saigon came under attack. Viet Cong blew up ammunition stored at Long Binh, the American headquarters for Saigon. Viet Cong also attacked the Saigon airport and the U.S. air base at Bien Hoa, about 15 miles (24 kilometers) north of Saigon. Communist forces outside Saigon fought to keep the Americans from sending troops into the city.

Once the attacks began, the teams in Saigon did not communicate with each other. Some teams seized their target and waited for NVA forces that never came. Others

*Major Tet Offensive battles occurred in or near Saigon.*

were killed when they attacked. By morning, American
planes and tanks had blasted the Viet Cong forces
around the bases. But small teams of Viet Cong continued

fighting in Saigon for another 10 days. Elsewhere the gun battles continued for days. Civilians fled the cities by the thousands.

Though many of the Tet attacks failed, the fighting in Saigon caught the attention of the American people. They saw television film of the gun battle for the embassy, the 15-hour battle against the Viet Cong near the Presidential Palace, and the fires from burning planes and ammunition at the bases.

The sudden attacks and the color photographs and film of destruction shocked most Americans. They had believed President Johnson when he had told them the Viet Cong were losing the Tet battles. News reporters had told viewers what they knew, but in the heat of battle, the stories were often wrong. When the inaccurate reports were later corrected, most Americans did not notice. They were watching and reading new reports of bloody battles.

By February 10, most South Vietnamese cities were quiet again. But the fighting still raged in two areas.

**27**

*Wounded Marines were carried away from Hue on a tank. Images of dead and injured U.S. troops shocked and upset many Americans.*

American reporters flocked to the northern city of Hue and to the Khe Sanh base, where fighting continued. Bloody battles still appeared on the evening news.

# THE BATTLE FOR HUE

The imperial city of Hue had once been the home of Vietnamese emperors. The center of the city was a walled citadel, a fort built to protect the emperor from attack. Surrounded by a moat and topped by towers, the citadel looked like a castle. About half of the city lay within the citadel walls. Hue had been peaceful for most of the war, and only a few ARVN troops were based there.

At 3:30 A.M. on January 31, the NVA and Viet Cong launched

*The royal citadel in Hue was built in 1804.*

their attack in Hue. The communists hammered the city with artillery and sent troops racing into the city. Crossing the moats and firing their weapons, they quickly took the citadel. South Vietnam's General Ngo Quang Truong ordered his soldiers to defend their headquarters in the

*General Ngo Quang Truong was in charge of the headquarters at Hue.*

citadel. But many soldiers had gone home for Tet, and Truong could not stop the communist forces.

South of the citadel, the U.S. Military Assistance Command was located in a walled compound. About 200 American military advisers and other soldiers jumped into bunkers as the artillery struck their building. The bunkers protected the soldiers from bombs and shells. No other American soldiers were stationed in Hue. By morning, the communist forces controlled all of the city except the U.S. command and ARVN headquarters.

The communist soldiers carried lists of enemies to capture or kill. South Vietnamese military officers, government officials, teachers, and foreigners were on the lists. Teams of Viet Cong soldiers moved through the captured neighborhoods. They ordered the targeted people out of their homes. Some were killed on the spot, and many others were killed later. Mass graves held nearly 3,000 bodies.

On the south side of Hue, more than 400 South Vietnamese men took shelter in a cathedral. The communist

*A destroyed bridge did not stop civilians from crossing the Perfume River to escape the violence in Hue.*

troops ordered them to come out. They marched the men out of Hue. More than a year later, their mass grave was found about 10 miles (16 km) outside of the city.

32

General Truong radioed for all nearby ARVN troops to return to Hue. NVA forces outside the city kept them from coming in. Fighting fiercely, the ARVN troops finally arrived at headquarters on the afternoon of February 1. Marines were also sent to help the U.S. military advisers at the command center. About 200 Marines fought their way into the city from the south. They had arrived at the U.S. command the previous day.

The Marines and General Truong coordinated their plans. The Marines would attack the south side of the citadel, while the ARVN troops would attack from the north. By this time, the communist soldiers were in position on top of the citadel's 30-foot (9-m) walls. The walls were their greatest advantage. They could fire at the Americans from above, then hide behind the rock walls to avoid return fire. It took more than a week for the Marines to take four city blocks in front of the citadel walls.

Over the next three weeks, the Marines and ARVN soldiers used all the firepower they had. Artillery, helicopter

*Positioned behind the citadel wall, a U.S. Marine tank rolled through a residential area.*

gunships, and heavy guns on U.S. Navy ships in the South China Sea pounded the citadel and the remaining communist troops. By February 13, nearly every building in Hue was damaged or destroyed. A Marine described what he saw: "My first impression was of desolation, utter devastation. There were burnt-out tanks and trucks, upturned automobiles still smoldering. Bodies lay everywhere, most of them civilians."

On February 25, ARVN soldiers tore down the North Vietnamese flag above the citadel and raised their own. The battle had lasted 25 days, and it left 80 percent of Hue residents with damaged or destroyed homes. More than 5,000 civilians were listed as dead or missing. The people of Hue moved into refugee camps and began to bury their dead.

*The citadel was severely damaged before the battle ended and the South Vietnam flag was raised.*

**35**

During the battle for Hue, American reporters had camped out in the citadel. They sent daily reports and film back to the United States. Many interviewed Marines in the middle of the battle. The reporters saw the bloody fighting and reported it. It was also reported that on February 1, U.S. military officials had predicted it would take only a few days to take Hue back. The television reports about the battle convinced many Americans that the U.S. government was lying about the enemy attacks.

Meanwhile, the Marines still held the base at Khe Sanh, but NVA artillery continued to shell it daily. Many days the Marines did not get enough food, water, or ammunition. General Westmoreland called in B-52 bombers, each of which carried more than 50,000 pounds (22,500 kilograms) of bombs. The heavy U.S. bombing killed thousands of NVA soldiers at Khe Sanh.

At the end of March, the NVA soldiers began to leave. On April 1, Westmoreland sent Army troops to clear the road to Khe Sanh and deal with the last of the NVA

*B-52 bombers were used to drop more than 15,000 tons (13,500 metric tons) of bombs on North Vietnam, Cambodia, and Laos during the Vietnam War.*

troops. A general was amazed at the destruction from artillery and bombs. "The place was absolutely denuded [bare]," he said. "The trees were gone … everything was gone." On April 8, the Army relieved the Marines at Khe Sanh. The Marines had held the base for 77 days.

# The Importance of the Tet Offensive

The Tet Offensive changed how many Americans felt about the Vietnam War. They had mostly supported the war before January 1968. Though some protested against the war, most Americans wanted the United States to win in Vietnam. They wanted to prevent the spread of communism.

As Americans watched the television news reports and read the newspapers during the Tet Offensive, many began to see the war as a waste of men and money. They believed the war could not be won. President Johnson had considered sending more troops, bombing more targets, and invading North Vietnam. Now none of the choices seemed like a good one to most Americans.

During a televised speech on March 31, 1968, President Johnson said he had decided to push North Vietnam for peace negotiations. He promised to stop bombing North Vietnam if their leaders agreed to talk about an

CBS Evening News *anchor Walter Cronkite hosted a special news report from Vietnam, covering the aftermath of the Tet Offensive.*

end to the war. "There is no need to delay talks that could

bring an end to this long and bloody war," Johnson said.

Then he surprised many people by announcing that

*Though the United States and South Vietnam had won the battles of the Tet Offensive, President Johnson's popularity plummeted along with Americans' support for the war.*

he would not run for another term as president. He was

being challenged for the presidency from within his own

political party. And recent opinion polls had shown that

only 26 percent of Americans approved of his handling

of the war.

Most historians agree that the communists lost

the battles of the Tet Offensive. They did not hold any

cities, and the South Vietnamese did not rise against their government. Worst of all, the communists lost as many as 50,000 NVA and Viet Cong soldiers. The Viet Cong were no longer considered a military threat, and the Vietnamese increasingly saw the war as one of North versus South.

Despite the American and ARVN victories, many Americans no longer believed in their leaders or in the war. After the war, North Vietnamese General Tran Do admitted that the Tet Offensive had not achieved its military goals. But he called the change in American opinion about the war "a fortunate result." Most Americans were no longer willing to fight a war for South Vietnam. But it would be another five years before the last U.S. troops left.

# GLOSSARY

**artillery**—large weapons, such as cannons or missile launchers, that require several soldiers to load, aim, and fire

**cease-fire**—period of time during a war when both sides agree to stop fighting

**citadel**—fortress built to protect a city

**civilian**—person who is not in the military

**embassy**—office for a country's representatives in another country

**guerrilla**—soldier who is not part of a regular army; guerrillas often use surprise attacks against an enemy

**negotiate**—bargain for an agreement between two countries, such as an end to a war

**offensive**—military attack

**stalemate**—situation in which neither side of opposing forces can win

**Viet Cong**—common name for communist guerrillas of South Vietnam who wanted it to reunite with North Vietnam

# DID YOU KNOW?

- The deadliest day of the entire Vietnam War for Americans was the second day of the Tet Offensive. On January 31, 1968, 245 U.S. soldiers died.

- The Vietnam War is often called the first television war. By 1968, all the major U.S. television networks had offices in Saigon. Reporters sent film of battles and destruction to the United States via satellite, often on the same day the battles occurred. Before the Vietnam War, Americans only read newspapers and magazines or viewed photographs and newsreels to find out about wars.

- Throughout the Vietnam War, North Vietnam sent men and supplies to South Vietnam on the Ho Chi Minh Trail. North Vietnamese General Giap described it after the war as a system of roads, gas pipelines, and communication systems. Workers had to repair the roads after frequent bombings by the United States.

- The Marine base at Khe Sanh was important to U.S. leaders during the Tet Offensive. Yet military leaders decided to abandon the base in June 1968. Historians are not sure why the base was defended for 77 days but was not important three months later.

# IMPORTANT DATES

## Timeline

| 1965 | In March, the first U.S. combat troops arrive in South Vietnam. |
| 1967 | In July, North Vietnam's leaders begin planning the Tet Offensive. |
| 1968 | First attack at Khe Sanh on January 21; on January 30, six South Vietnamese cities are hit in the first Tet attacks; the next day, more than 100 additional cities in South Vietnam are attacked; on February 25, American and ARVN troops recapture Hue; on March 31, President Johnson announces he will not run for another term as president; on April 8, the U.S. Army breaks the siege at Khe Sanh. |
| 1969 | President Richard Nixon announces the first U.S. troop withdrawals. |
| 1970 | U.S. troop strength in Vietnam is about 280,000. |
| 1973 | A cease-fire is declared, and U.S. troops leave Vietnam. |

# IMPORTANT PEOPLE

## Ngo Quang Truong (1929–2007)

*South Vietnamese general who defended his headquarters in the citadel of Hue; when South Vietnam fell in 1975, Truong immigrated to the United States; he wrote two books about the Vietnam War and became a U.S. citizen in 1983*

## Nguyen Van Thieu (1923–2001)

*Joined the Vietnamese army in the 1940s; served as president of South Vietnam from 1967 to 1975; distrusted the American will to protect South Vietnam and repeatedly refused to negotiate with North Vietnam; fled Vietnam just before Saigon fell, in April 1975*

## Vo Nguyen Giap (1912– )

*North Vietnamese general who planned the battle that defeated the French in 1954; planned the Tet Offensive and most of the other military attacks against U.S. and South Vietnamese forces during the Vietnam War; retired after the final battle to unify Vietnam*

## William C. Westmoreland (1914–2005)

*Served in World War II and the Korean War; was appointed to head the Vietnam military advisory mission in 1964; served as general in command of U.S. combat forces in Vietnam from 1964 to 1968; served as the Army's chief of staff from 1968 until he retired in 1972*

# WANT TO KNOW MORE?

## More Books to Read

Burgan, Michael. *The Vietnam War.* Milwaukee: World Almanac
Library, 2007.

Caputo, Philip. *10,000 Days of Thunder: A History of the Vietnam War.*
New York: Atheneum, 2005.

Gibson, Karen Bush. *The Vietnam War.* Hockessin, Del.: Mitchell Lane
Publishers, 2007.

Murray, Stuart. *Vietnam War.* New York: DK Publishing, 2005.

Worth, Richard. *Tet Offensive.* Broomall, Pa.: Chelsea House, 2002.

## On the Web

For more information on this topic, use FactHound.

1. Go to *www.facthound.com*

2. Type in this book ID: 0756538440

3. Click on the *Fetch It* button.

FactHound will find the best Web sites for you.

## On the Road

**National Vietnam Veterans**
**Art Museum**
1801 S. Indiana Ave.
Chicago, IL 60616
312/326-0270
An exhibit of more than 1,500 works
of art done by more than 100 artists
who have expressed their thoughts
and experiences of the Vietnam War

**Vietnam Veterans Memorial**
National Mall
Washington, DC
202/426-6841
National monument that honors
troops killed or missing in Vietnam;
Vietnam Women's Memorial is
nearby

**Look for more We the People books about this era:**

*The 19th Amendment*
*The Berlin Airlift*
*The Civil Rights Act of 1964*
*The Draft Lottery*
*The Dust Bowl*
*Ellis Island*
*The Fall of Saigon*
*GI Joe in World War II*
*The Great Depression*
*The Holocaust Museum*
*The Kent State Shootings*
*The Korean War*
*The My Lai Massacre*

*Navajo Code Talkers*
*The Negro Leagues*
*Pearl Harbor*
*The Persian Gulf War*
*The San Francisco Earthquake of 1906*
*Selma's Bloody Sunday*
*September 11*
*The Sinking of the USS Indianapolis*
*The Statue of Liberty*
*The Titanic*
*The Tuskegee Airmen*
*Vietnam Veterans Memorial*
*Vietnam War POWs*

A complete list of We the People titles is available on our Web site:
www.compasspointbooks.com

**47**

# INDEX

### About the Author

Mary Englar is a freelance writer and a teacher of English and creative writing. She has a master of fine arts degree in writing from Minnesota State University, Mankato, and has written more than 30 nonfiction books for children. She continues to read and write about the many different cultures of our world in Minnesota.